AMERICAN LANGUAGE REPRINTS

VOL. 25

OBSERVATIONS ON THE MAHICAN LANGUAGE

by
Jonathan Edwards

Evolution Publishing
Merchantville, New Jersey

Reprinted from:

Jonathan Edwards. 1788. *Observations on the Language of the Muhhekaneew Indians*. New Haven: Josiah Meigs.

This edition ©2002 by Evolution Publishing.
an imprint of Arx Publishing, LLC

Originally published in hardcover 2002.
Reprinted in paperback 2025.

Printed in the
United States of America

ISSN 1540-3475

ISBN 978-1-935228-35-6

CONTENTS

Preface to the 2002 edition 1

Preface to the 1788 edition 9

Observations, &c..11

Mahican—English 29

English—Mahican 37

Numerical Table..43

Classification Table...45

Preface to the 2002 edition

There has been confusion for many years surrounding two different American tribes of geographical and linguistic proximity. The first of these, the *Mahicans*, inhabited the Hudson River Valley in upstate New York, and came to be known by the English as "River Indians" ; the second tribe, the *Mohegans*, lived aboriginally along the banks of the Connecticut River, and were closely related to the Pequot, whom they conquered in the 1630s. When, for example, James Fenimore Cooper wrote his *Last of the Mohicans* he was referring to the Hudson Valley tribe, but Uncas, the character to whom the title refers, takes the name from a famous Connecticut chief of the 1600s.

Since the English names are so similar as to be nearly identical, nowadays scholars delineate the two tribes with a careful distinction in spelling. Though these distinctions are often blurred, particularly in older sources, Mahican/Mohican, the forms with 'c', are used to refer to the Hudson Valley Algonquians and are the subject of the present volume.

Mahican is an Eastern Algonquian language, intermediate between its relatives to the north (Western Abenaki, Nipmuck-Pocumtuck or Loup, Quiripi and Mohegan-Pequot), and those to the south (Minsi and Unami Delaware). Overall it shows a somewhat closer relation to Delaware than the New England languages, for which reason modern classifications have placed Mahican in a Delawaran subfamily (Goddard 1996).

1

Two dialects have been named based on the two most prominent Mahican groups in the 18th and 19th centuries. The Moravian dialect, with roots in Dutchess County NY, is named for the German-speaking Moravian missionaries who documented it in the 1700s: David Zeisberger, Johann Jacob Schmick, and Ernestus Heckewelder. The Stockbridge dialect, from the Massachusetts town of the same name, was recorded by Englishmen and native Mahicans: Jonathan Edwards, John Quinney, Hendrick Aupaumut and William Jenks. There are also extensive 20th century manuscripts in Stockbridge by Truman Michelson and Morris Swadesh, housed respectively in the libraries of the Bureau of American Ethnology and the American Philosophical Society.

No comprehensive analysis of Mahican dialectology has yet been published. However, Warne's (1980) comparison between "Old Mahican" and "Modern Mahican," through analysis of the historical development of the language, effectively delineates the two dialects as well, since the former is based on Moravian and the latter was based on the Stockbridge data of the early 20th century. After some of the later developments are accounted for, there remain a few minor distinctions between Stockbridge and Moravian, but it is not yet known how these differences relate to aboriginal Mahican geography.

The earliest existing source on the Stockbridge dialect is also without a doubt the best known of all the historical sources of Mahican: Jonathan Edwards' *Observations on the Language of the Muhhekaneew Indians*. Submitted for publication to the Connecticut Society of Arts and Sciences on October 23rd, 1787, the *Observations* made it into print the following year. One of the foremost modern Algonquianists called this work "perhaps the most significant grammar of a North American language published in the eighteenth century," (Goddard 1996), and upon reading the preface it is not hard to see why.

Unlike most other white linguists of the time period, Edwards had a native command of the language he was describing. Son of a missionary preacher, he had lived among the Indians at Stockbridge since he was six years old, and outside the confines of his home "seldom heard any language spoken, beside the Indian." Through constant use he apparently developed a native fluency, an accomplishment that, according to his Mahican neighbors, had never before been achieved by any Anglo-American.

Such a singular background alone would have qualified Edwards to produce extraordinary work. Yet he wisely supplemented his native ear with an extra step of scholarly carefulness, and had a draft of the *Observations* read and corrected by one of the Mahican leaders at Stockbridge.

A modern linguist could hardly dare to ask for any more beneficial circumstances for early data—though might certainly wish Edwards had gone into more detail. From a descriptive standpoint, the *Observations* are certainly too brief; they hardly cover even the most elementary features of Mahican grammar. But as is evident from the title of his work, it was not Edwards' intention to produce a full-fledged description of Mahican—his scope

3

was much more modest and his interests were somewhat more theoretical and polemical.

As it is all too easy to undervalue the scientific insights of a previous age, Edwards' understanding of historical and comparative linguistics deserves special mention. Only one year after Sir William Jones' famous statements concerning the existence of a proto-Indo-European language, Edwards presented evidence that Shawnee and Chippewa, like many other languages (see p. 11), were "radically the same" as Mahican and concluded from this similarity that "they are mere dialects of the same original language"—essentially describing what we know today as proto-Algonquian. That he was referring to true genetic relationships and not just superficial and coincidental "affinities" is proved by his specific exclusion of Mohawk, which he called "entirely different" from Mahican, and dismissed either's derivation from the other.

Yet such keen scientific insight only makes his suggestive comparisons with Hebrew appear even more out of place. At the time, there was a widespread hypothesis that the American Indians were remnants of the ten lost tribes of Israel. And while Edwards was personally inclined to agreeing with the connection, and presented some supporting evidence for it, he ultimately remained cautious about any linguistic proof. Within a few decades a more fully-developed linguistic science was able to better distinguish genetic relationships from chance similarities, and the Algonquian family's linear descent from Hebrew was thus wholly disproven.

In this new edition, Edwards' treatise has been repub-

lished in its entirety; the spelling and the overall formatting of the original have been retained. Note that (modern usage notwithstanding) Edwards regularly writes "Mohegan" instead of "Mahican," though his uncorrupted form in the native pronunciation, *Muhhekaneew*, is the ultimate source of the latter. His orthography, as with all the early recordings of Stockbridge Mahican, is English, and uses no invented symbols or unusual diacritical markings.

In a later annotated reprint of the *Observations* (Pickering 1823), the editor corresponded with Edwards' son "for the purpose of obtaining the use of a revised copy, if any such existed." No such revision, though, was ever made by Edwards, nor was his son able to find the original manuscript. The younger Edwards believed that the printing was "probably pretty free from errours," since his father had personally inspected the first printed copies. Nevertheless, he did inform Pickering of three minor emendations in his father's handwriting, two of which were corrections of Mahican words. These emendations have been incorporated into the present edition.

The original printing of the *Observations* was somewhat uneven in its use of italics to mark non-English words; for the sake of consistency and clarity, I have set all these in italics. Also, in keeping with the format of this series, two alphabetized Mahican and English glossaries have also been added, recapitulating all 150 of the Mahican terms defined in the text (not counting those of the *Our Father*). A numerical table has also been added immediately subsequent to these.

The Stockbridge dialect of Mahican was still spoken into the 1930s, outlasting its Moravian counterpart which became extinct sometime in the 19th century (Goddard 1978, Masthay 1991). In the years after Edwards lived among them, more than 400 Mahican had left Stockbridge for Central New York State, where they founded New Stockbridge on lands granted them by the Oneida. Then in the early 1820s, John Pickering received a letter from the town missionary informing him that "the Stockbridge tribe, with the Six Nations, have obtained a fine country in the vicinity of Green Bay; and eventually they will emigrate thither in the course of a few years" (Pickering 1823). This relocation to Shawano County, Wisconsin, would be their last, and there the Stockbridge descendants remain today.

A few important works of Mahican linguistics have been published in the last two decades (Masthay 1980, Masthay 1991, Warne 1980), but ironically the most modern materials have never seen publication; nor has there been any modern analysis of the older Stockbridge texts (see Walker 1996). Mahican linguistics, therefore, suffers only from the obscurity of its sources and not from any lack of data, creating a wide potential for research in the years to come.

—Claudio R. Salvucci, series ed.

Bibliography and Recommended Reading

Brasser, T.J. 1978. "Mahican" in William Sturtevant, Bruce Trigger, eds., *Handbook of North American Indians vol. 15: Northeast*, pp. 198-212. Washington D.C.:Smithsonian Institution.

Edwards, Tryon. *The Works of Jonathan Edwards, D.D. late president of Union College, With a memoir of his life and character.* Various publishers.

Foster, Michael K. 1996. "Language and the culture history of North America." in William Sturtevant, Ives Goddard, eds., *Handbook of North American Indians vol. 17: Languages*, pp. 64-110, esp. "Algic" pp.97-100. Washington D.C.:Smithsonian Institution.

Goddard, Ives. 1978. "Eastern Algonquian Languages" in William Sturtevant, Bruce Trigger, eds., *Handbook of North American Indians vol. 15: Northeast*, pp. 70-77. Washington D.C.:Smithsonian Institution.

Goddard, Ives. 1996. "Introduction" in William Sturtevant, Ives Goddard, eds., *Handbook of North American Indians vol. 17: Languages*, pp. 1-16. Washington D.C.:Smithsonian Institution.

Masthay, Carl, ed. 1980. *Mahican-language Hymns, Biblical Prose, and Vocabularies from Moravian Sources, with 11 Mohawk Hymns.* St. Louis, Missouri.

Masthay, Carl, ed. 1991. *Schmick's Mahican Dictionary.* Memoirs of the American Philosophical Society, Volume 197. Philadelphia.

Pentland, David H. 1991. "Mahican Historical Phonology." in Masthay, ed. *Schmick's Mahican Dictionary*, pp. 15-27. Memoirs of the American Philosophical Society, Volume 197. Philadelphia.

Pickering, John, ed. 1823. "Doctor Edwards' Observations on the Mohegan Language", pp. 81-160 in *Collections of the Massachusetts Historical Society*, Second series, Volume 10. Boston.

Prince, J. Dyneley. 1905. "A Tale in the Hudson River Indian Language." *American Anthropologist*, n.s. 7(1):74-84.

Walker, Willard B. 1996. "Native Writing Systems" in William Sturtevant, Ives Goddard, eds., *Handbook of North American Indians vol. 17: Languages*, pp. 158-184. Washington D.C.:Smithsonian Institution.

Warne, Janet L. 1980. "Time-depth in Mahican diachronic phonology: evidence from the Schmick manuscript." In William Cowan, ed., *Papers of the 11th Algonquian Conference* (Ottawa:Carelton University), 166-182.

Preface to the 1788 Edition

That the following observations may obtain credit, it may be proper to inform the reader, with what advantages they have been made.

When I was but six years of age, my father removed with his family to Stockbridge, *which at that time, was inhabited by Indians almost solely; as there were in the town but twelve families of whites or Anglo-Americans, and perhaps one hundred and fifty families of Indians. The Indians being the nearest neighbours, I constantly associated with them; their boys were my daily school-mates and play-fellows. Out of my father's house, I seldom heard any language spoken, beside the Indian. By these means I acquired the knowledge of that language, and a great facility in speaking it. It became more familiar to me than my mother tongue. I knew the names of some things in Indian, which I did not know in English; even all my thoughts ran in Indian: and though the true pronunciation of the language is extremely difficult to all but themselves, the acknowledged, that I had acquired it perfectly; which as they said, never had been acquired before by any Anglo-American. On account of this acquisition, as well as on account of my skill in their language in general, I received from them many compliments applauding my superior wisdom. This skill in their language I have in a good measure retained to this day.*

After I had drawn up these observations, lest there should be some mistakes in them, I carried them to Stockbridge, and read them to Capt. Yōghum, *a principal*

Indian of the tribe, who is well versed in his own language, and tolerably informed concerning the English: and I availed myself of his remarks and corrections.

From these facts, the reader will form his own opinion of the truth and accuracy of what is now offered him

When I was in my tenth year, my father sent me among the six nations, with a design that I should learn their language, and thus become qualified to be a missionary among them. But on account of the war with France, which then existed, I continued among them but about six months. Therefore the knowledge which I acquired of that language was but imperfect; and at this time I retain so little of it, that I will not hazard any particular critical remarks on it. I may observe however, that though the words of the two languages are totally different, yet their structure is in some respects analogous, particularly in the use of prefixes and suffixes.

Observations, &c.

The language which is now the subject of observation is that of the *Muhhekaneew* or Stockbridge Indians. They, as well as the tribe at New-London, are by the Anglo-Americans, called *Mohegans*, which is a corruption of *Muhhekaneew**, in the singular, or *Muhhekaneok* in the plural. This language is spoken by all the Indians throughout New-England. Every tribe, as that of Stockbridge, that of Farmington, that of New-London &c, has a different dialect; but the language is radically the same. Mr. Elliot's translation of the bible is in a particular dialect of this language. The dialect followed in these observations, is that of Stockbridge. This language appears to be much more extensive than any other language in North-America. The languages of the Delawares, in Pennsylvania, of the Penobscots bordering on Nova-Scotia, of the Indians of St. Francis in Canada, of the Shawanese on the Ohio, and of the Chippewaus at the westward of lake Huron, are all radically the same with the Mohegan. The same is said concerning the languages of the Ottowaus, Nanticooks, Munsees, Menomonees, Messisaugas, Saukies, Ottagaumies, Killistinoes, Nipegons, Algonkins, Winnebagoes, &c. That the languages of the several tribes in New-England, of the Delawares, and of Mr. Elliot's bible, are radically the same with the Mohegan, I assert from my own knowledge.

What I assert concerning the language of the

---

* Wherever *w* occurs in an Indian word, it is a mere consonant, as in *work*, *world*, &c.

11

Penobscots, I have from a Gentleman in Massachusetts, who has been much conversant among the Indians. That the languages of the Shawanese and Chippewaus is radically the same with the Mohegan, I shall endeavour to shew. My authorities for what I say of the languages of the other nations are Capt. *Yoghum*, before mentioned, and *Carver's travels*.

To illustrate the analogy between the *Mohegan*, the *Shawanee*, and the *Chippewau* languages, I shall exhibit a short list of words of those three languages. For the list of *Mohegan* words I myself am accountable. That of the *Shawanee* words was communicated to me by General *Parsons*, who has had opportunity to make a partial vocabulary of that language. For the words of the *Chippewau* language I am dependent on *Carver's Travels*.

English.	*Mohegan.*	*Shawanee.*
A Bear	Mquoh	Mauquah
A beaver	Amisque*	Amaquah
Eye	Hkeesque	Skeesacoo
Ear	Towohque	Towacah
Fetch	Pautoh	Peatoloo
My Grandfather	Nemoghhome†	Nemasompethau
My Grandmother	Nohhum	Nocumthau
My Granchild	Naughees	Noosthethau
He goes	Pumissoo	Pomthalo
A girl	Peesquausoo	Squauthauthau
House	Weekumuhm	Weecuah

* *e* final is never sounded in any Indian word, which I write, except monosyllables.

† *gh* in any Indian word has the strong guttural sound, which is given by the Scots to the same letters in *tough*, *enough*, &c.

12

He (that man)	Uwoh	Welah
His head	Weensis	Weeseh (I imagine misspelt, for weenseh.)
His heart	Utoh	Otaheh
Hair	Weghaukun	Welathoh
Her husband	Waughecheh	Wasecheh
His teeth	Wepeeton	Wepeetalee
I thank you	Wneeweh	Neauweh
My uncle	Nsees	Neeseethau
I	Neah	Nelah
Thou	Keah	Kelah
We	Neaunuh	Nelauweh
Ye	Keauwuh	Kelauweh
Water	Nbey	Nippee
Elder sister	Nmees	Nemeethau
River	Sepoo	Thepee

The following is a specimen of analogy between the Mohegan and Chippewau languages.

English	Mohegan	Chippiwau.
A bear	Mquoh	Mackwah
A beaver	Amisque	Amik
To die (I die)	Nip	Nip
Dead (he is dead)	Nboo or nepoo*	Neepoo
Devil	Mtandou, or Mannito†	Manitou
Dress the kettle (make a fire)	Pootouwah	Poutwah
His eyes	Ukeesquan	Wiskinkhie

* The first syllable scarcely sounded.
† The last of these words properly signifies a spectre or any thing frightful.

13

Fire	Stauw	Scutta
Give it him	Meenuh	Millaw
A spirit (a spectre)	Mannito	Manitou
How	Tuneh ‡	Tawnè
House	Weekumuhm	Wigwaum
An impostor (he is an impostor or bad man)	Mtissoo	Mawlawtissie
Go	Pumisseh	Pimmoussie
Marry	Weeween	Weewin
Good for nought	Mtit	Malatat
River	Sepoo	Sippim
Shoe	Mkissin	Maukissin
The sun	Keesogh	Kissis
Sit down	Mattipeh	Mintipin
Water	Nbey	Nebbi
Where	Tehah	Tah
Winter	Hpoon	Pepoun
Wood	Metooque	Mittic

Almost every man who writes Indian words, spells them in a peculiar manner: and I dare say, if the same person had taken down all the words above, from the mouth of the Indians, he would have spelt them more alike, and the coincidence would have appeared more striking. Most of those who write and print Indian words, use the letter *a* where the sound is that of *oh* or *au*. Hence the reader will observe, that in some of the Mohegan words above, *o* or *oh* is used, when *a* or *ah* is used in the correspondent words of the other languages: as *Mquoh, Mauquah*. I

‡ Whenever *u* occurs, it has not the long sound of the English *u* as in *commune*; but the sound of *u* in *uncle*, though much protracted. The other vowels are to be pronounced, as in English.

14

doubt not the sound of those two syllables is exactly the same, as pronounced by the Indians of the different tribes.

It is not to be supposed, that the like coincidence is extended to all the words of those languages. Very many words are totally different. Still the analogy is such as is sufficient to show, that they are mere dialects of the same original language.

I could not throughout, give words of the same signification in the three languages, as the two vocabularies, from which I extracted the *Shawanee* and *Chippewau* words, did not contain words of the same signification, excepting in some instances.

The Mohauk, which is the language of the six nations is entirely different from that of the Mohegans. There is no more appearance of a derivation of one of these last mentioned languages from the other, than there is of a derivation of either of them from the English. One obvious diversity, and in which the Mohauk is perhaps different from every other language, is, that it is wholly destitute of labials: whereas the Mohegan abounds with labials. I shall here give the numerals, as far as ten, and the *Pater noster*, in both languages.

Mohegan	*Mohauk*
Ngwittoh	Uskot
Neesoh	Teggeneh
Noghhoh	Ohs
Nauwoh	Kialeh
Nunon	Wisk
Ngwittus	Yoiyok

Tupouwus	Chautok
Ghusooh	Sottago
Nauneeweh	Teuhtoh
Mtannit	Wialeh

The Pater noster in the Mohegan language, is as follows;

Noghnuh, ne spummuck oieon, taugh mauweh wneh wtukoseauk neanne annuwoieon. Taugh ne aunchuwutammun wawehtuseek maweh noh pummeh. Ne annoihitteech mauweh awauneek noh hkey oiecheek, ne aunchuwutammun, ne aunoihitteet neek spummuk oiecheek. Menenaunuh noonooh wuhkamauk tquogh nuh uhhuyutamauk ngummauweh. Ohquutamouwenaunuh auneh mumachoieaukeh, ne anneh ohquutamouwoieauk numpeh neek mumacheh annehoquaukeek. Cheen hquukquaucheh siukeh annehenaunuh. Panneeweh htouwenaunuh neen maumtehkeh. Keah ngwehcheh kwiouwauweh mauweh noh pummeh; ktanwoi; estah awaun wtinnoiyuwun ne aunoieyon; hanweeweh ne ktinnoieen. Amen.

The Pater Noster, in the language of the Six Nations, taken from Smith's history of New-York, is this;

Soungwauneha caurounkyawga tehseetaroan sauhsoneyousta esa sawaneyou okettauhsela ehneauwoung na caurounkyawga nughwonshauga neatewehnesalauga taugwaunautoronoantoughsick toantaugweleewheyoustaung cheneeyeut chaquataulehwheyoustaunna toughsou taugwaussareneh tawautottenaugaloughtoungga nasawne sacheautaugwass coantehsalohaunzaickaw esa sawauneyou esa sashoutzta esa soungwasoung chenneauhaungwa; auwen.

16

The reader will observe, that there is not a single labial in either the numerals or the Pater noster of this language; and that when they come to *amen*, from an aversion to shutting the lips, they change the *m* to *w*.

In no part of these languages does there appear to be a greater coincidence, than in this specimen. I have never noticed one word in either of them, which has any analogy to the correspondent word in the other language.

Concerning the Mohegan language, it is observable, that there is no diversity of gender, either in nouns or pronouns. The very same words express *he* and *she*, *him* and *her*. Hence when the Mohegans speak English, they generally in this respect follow strictly their own idiom: A man will say concerning his wife, *he sick*, *he gone away*, &c.

With regard to *cases*, they have but one variation from the nominative, which is formed by the addition of the syllable *an* as *wnechun*, his child, *wnechunan*. This varied case seems to suit indifferently any case, except the nominative.

The plural is formed by adding a letter or syllable to the singular; as *nemannauw*, a man, *nemannauk*, men; *penumpausoo*, a boy, *penumpausoouk*, boys.

The Mohegans more carefully distinguish the natural relations of men to each other, than we do, or perhaps any other nation. They have one word to express an elder brother, *netohcon*; another to express a younger brother, *ngheesum*. One to express an elder sister, *nmase*; another to express a younger sister, *ngheesum*. But the word for younger brother and younger sister is the same,—*Nsase* is

17

my uncle by my mother's side: *nuchehque* is my uncle by the father's side.

The Mohegans have no adjectives in all their language; unless we reckon numerals and such words as *all*, *many*, &c. adjectives. Of adjectives which express the qualities of substances, I do not find that they have any. They express those qualities by verbs neuter; as *wnissoo*, he is beautiful, *mtissoo*, he is homely; *pehtuhquissoo*, he is tall; *nsconmoo*, he is malicious &c. Thus in Latin many qualities are expressed by verbs neuter, as *valeo*, *caleo*, *frigeo* &c. — Although it may at first, seem not only singular, and curious, but impossible, that a language should exist without adjectives; yet it is an indubitable fact. Nor do they seem to suffer any inconvenience by it. They as readily express any quality by a neuter verb, as we do by an adjective.

If it should be enquired, how it appears that the words above mentioned are not adjectives: I answer it appears, as they have all the same variations and declensions of other verbs. *To walk* will be acknowledged to be a verb. This verb is declined thus; *npumseh*, I walk; *kpumseh*, thou walkest; *pumissoo*, he walketh; *npumsehnuh*, we walk; *kpumsehmuh*, ye walk; *pumissoouk*, they walk. In the same manner are the words in question declined; *npehtuhquisseh*, I am tall; *kpehtuhquisseh*, thou art tall; *pehtuhquissoo*, he is tall; *npehtuhquissehnuh*, we are tall; *kpehtuhquissehmuh*, ye are tall; *pehtuhquessoouk*, they are tall.

Though the Mohegans have no proper adjectives, they have participles to all their verbs: as *pehtuhquisseet*, the man who is tall, *paumseet*, the man who walks; *waunseet*, the man who is beautiful; *oieet*, the man who lives or dwells in a place; *oioteet*, the man who fights. So in the plural, *pehtuhquisseecheek*, the tall men; *paumseecheek*, they who walk, &c.

It is observable of the participles of this language, that they are declined through the persons and numbers, in the same manner as verbs: thus, *paumse-uh*, I walking; *paumse-an*, thou walking; *paumseet*, he walking; *paumseauk*, we walking; *paumseauque*, ye walking; *paumse-cheek*, they walking.

They have no relative corresponding to our *who* or *which*. Instead of *the man who walks*, they say, the walking man, or the walker.

As they have no adjectives, of course they have no comparison of adjectives; yet they are put to no difficulty to express the comparative excellence or baseness of any two things. With a neuter verb expressive of the quality, they use an adverb to point out the degree: as *annuweeweh wnissoo*, he is more beautiful; *kahnuh wnissoo*, he is very beautiful. *Nemannauwoo*, he is a man: *annuweeweh nemannauwoo*, he is a man of superior excellence or courage; *kahnuh nemannnauwoo*, he is a man of extraordinary excellence or courage.

Beside the pronouns common in other languages, they express the pronouns both substantive and adjective, by *affixes*, or by letters or syllables added at the beginnings, or ends, or both, of their nouns. In this particular the structure of the language coincides with that of the Hebrew, in an instance in which the Hebrew differs from all the languages of Europe, antient or modern. However, the use of the affixed pronouns in the Mohegan language, is not perfectly similar to the use of them in the Hebrew. As in the Hebrew they are joined to the ends of words only, but in the Mohegan, they are sometimes joined to the ends, sometimes to the beginnings, and sometimes to both. Thus, *tmohhecan* is a hatchet or ax; *ndumhecan* is my hatchet; *ktumhecan*, thy hatchet; *utumhecan*, his hatchet; *ndumhecannuh*, our hatchet; *ktumhecanoowuh*, your hatchet; *utumhecannoowuh*, their hatchet. It is observable, that the pronouns for the singular number are prefixed, and for the plural, the prefixed pronouns for the singular being retained, there are others added as suffixes.

It is further to be observed, that by the increase of the word the vowels are changed and transposed; as *tmohecan*, *ndumhecan*; the *o* is changed into *u* and transposed, in a manner analogous to what is often done in the Hebrew. The *t* is changed into *d euphoniæ gratia*.

A considerable part of the appellatives are never used without a pronoun affixed. The Mohegans can say, my father, *nogh*, thy father, *kogh*, &c. &c. but they cannot say absolutely *father*. There is no such word in all their language. If you were to say *ogh*, which the word would be, if stripped of all affixes, you would make a Mohegan both stare and smile. The same observation is applicable to *mother*, *brother*, *sister*, *son*, *head*, *hand*, *foot*, &c. in short to those things in general which necessarily in their natural state belong to some person. A hatchet is sometimes found without an owner, and therefore they sometimes have occasion to speak of it absolutely, or without refer-

20

ring it to an owner. But as a *head*, *hand*, &c. naturally belong to some person, and they have no occasion to speak of them without referring to the person to whom they belong; so they have no words to express them absolutely. This I presume is a peculiarity in which this language differs from all languages, which have ever yet come to the knowledge of the learned world.

The pronouns are in like manner prefixed and suffixed to verbs. The Mohegans never use a verb in the infinitive mood, or without a nominative or agent; and never use a verb transitive without expressing, both the agent and the object, correspondent to the nominative and accusative cases in Latin. Thus they can neither say, *to love*, nor *I love*, *thou givest* &c. But they can say, *I love thee*, *thou givest him*, &c. viz. *Nduhwhunuw* I love him or her; *nduhwhuntammin* I love it; *ktuhwhunin*, I love thee; *ktuhwhunoohmuh*, I love you, (in the plural) *nduhwhununk*, I love them. This, I think, is another peculiarity of this language.

Another peculiarity is, that the nominative and accusative pronouns prefixed and suffixed, are always used, even though other nominatives and accusatives be expressed. Thus they cannot say, *John loves Peter* ; they always say, *John he loves him Peter* ; *John uduhwhunuw Peteran.* Hence when the Indians begin to talk English, they universally express themselves according to this idiom.

It is further observable, that the pronoun in the accusative case is sometimes in the same instance expressed by both a prefix and a suffix; as *kthuwhunin*, I love thee. The *k* prefixed, and the syllable *in*, suffixed, both unite to

21

express, and are both necessary to express the accusative case *thee*.

They have no verb substantive in all the language. Therefore they cannot say, *he is a man, he is a coward* &c. They express the same by one word, which is a verb neuter, viz. *nemannauwoo*, he is a man. *Nemannauw* is the noun substantive, *man*: that turned into a verb neuter of the third person singular, becomes *nemannauwoo*, as in Latin it is said, *græcor, græcatur* &c. Thus they turn any substantive whatever into a verb neuter: as *kmattannis-sauteuh* you are a coward, from *matansautee*, a coward: *kpeesquausooeh*, you are a girl, from *peesquausoo*, a girl*.

Hence also we see the *reason*, why they have no verb substantive. As they have no adjectives, and as they turn their substantives into verbs on any occasion: they have no use for the substantive or auxiliary verb.

The third person singular seems to be the radix, or most simple form of the several persons of their verbs in the indicative mood: but the second person singular of the imperative, seems to be the most simple of any of the forms of their verbs: as *meetseh*, eat thou: *meetsoo*, he eateth: *nmeetseh*, I eat: *kmeetseh*, thou eatest &c.

They have a past and future tense to their verbs; but often, if not generally, they use the form of the present tense, to express both past and future events. As *wnuku-woh ndiotuwohpoh*, yesterday I fought; or *wnukuwoh ndiotuwoh*, yesterday I fight: *ndiotuwauch wupkoh*; I shall fight to-morrow or *wupkauch ndiotuwoh*, to-morrow I

---

* The circumstance that they have no verb substantive, accounts for their not using that verb, when they speak English. They say, *I man, I sick* &c.

fight. In this last case the variation of *wupkoh* to *wup-kauch* denotes the future tense; and this variation is in the word *to-morrow*, not in the verb *fight*.

They have very few prepositions, and those are rarely used, but in composition. *Anneh* is to, *ocheh* is from. But to, from, &c. are almost always expressed by an alteration of the verb. Thus, *ndoghpeh* is I ride, and *Wnoghquetookoke* is Stockbridge. But if I would say in Indian *I ride to Stockbridge*, I must say, not *anneh Wnoghquetookoke ndoghpeh*, but *Wnoghquetookoke ndinnetoghpeh*. If I would say, *I ride from Stockbridge*, it must be, not *ocheh Wnoghquetookoke ndoghpeh*; but *Wnoghquetookoke nochetoghpeh*. Thus *ndinnoghoh* is I walk to a place: *notoghoh* I walk from a place: *ndin-nehnuh*, I run to a place: *nochehnuh*, I run from a place. And any verb may be compounded, with the prepositions, *anneh* and *ocheh*, to and from.

It has been said, that savages have no parts of speech beside the substantive and the verb. This is not true concerning the Mohegans, nor concerning any other tribe of Indians, of whose language I have any knowledge. The Mohegans have all the eight parts of speech, to be found in other languages, though prepositions are so rarely used, except in composition, that I once determined that part of speech to be wanting. It has been said also, that savages never abstract, and have no abstract terms, which with regard to the Mohegans is another mistake. They have *uhwhundowukon*, love: *sekeenundowukon*, hatred: *nscon-mowukon*, malice: *peyuhtommauwukon*, religion, &c. I doubt not but that there is in this language the full proportion of abstract, to concrete terms, which is commonly to be found in other languages.

Besides what has been observed concerning prefixes and suffixes, there is a remarkable analogy, between some words in the Mohegan language, and the correspondent words in the Hebrew, — In Mohegan *Neah* is I: the Hebrew of which is *Ani*. *Keah* is thou or thee: the Hebrews use *ka* the suffix. *Uwoh* is this man, or this thing: very analogous to the Hebrew *hu* or *hua*, ipse. *Neaunuh* is we: in the Hebrew *nachnu* and *anachnu*.

In Hebrew *ni* is the suffix for *me*, or the first person. In the Mohegan *n* or *ne* is prefixed to denote the first person. As *nmeetseh* or *nemeetseh*, I eat. In Hebrew *k* or *ka* is the suffix for the second person, and is indifferently either a pronoun substantive or adjective. *K* or *ka* has the same use in the Mohegan language: as *kmeetseh* of *kameetseh*, thou eatest; *knisk*, thy hand. In Hebrew the *vau*, the letter *u* & *hu* are the suffixes for he or him. In Mohegan the same is expressed by *u* or *uw*, and by *oo*: as *nduhwhunuw*, I love him, *pumissoo*, he walketh. The suffix to express *our* or *us* in Hebrew is *nu*, in Mohegan the suffix of the same signification is *nuh*: as *noghnuh* our father: *nmeetsehnuh*, we eat, &c.

How far the use of prefixes and suffixes, together with these instances of analogy, and perhaps other instances, which may be traced out by those who have more leisure, go towards proving, that the North American Indians are of Hebrew, or at least Asiatic extraction, is submitted to the judgment of the learned. The facts are demonstrable; concerning the proper inferences every one will judge for himself. In the modern Armenian language, the pronouns are affixed*. How far affixes are in use among the other modern Asiatics, I have not had opportunity to obtain information. It is to be desired, that those who are informed, would communicate to the public what information they may possess, relating to this matter. Perhaps by such communication and by a comparison of the languages of the North-American Indians, with the languages of Asia, it may appear, not only from what quarter of the world, but from what particular nations, these Indians are derived.

It is to be wished, that every one who makes a vocabulary of any Indian language, would be careful to notice the prefixes and suffixes, and to distinguish accordingly. One man may ask an Indian, what he calls *hand* in his language, holding out his own hand to him. The Indian will naturally answer *knisk*, i.e. *thy* hand. Another man will ask the same question, pointing to the Indian's hand, In this case, he will naturally answer *nnisk*; *my* hand. Another may ask the same question, pointing to the hand of the third person. In this case, the answer will naturally be *unisk*, *his* hand. This would make a very considerable diversity in the corresponding words of different vocabularies; when if due attention were rendered to the personal prefixes and suffixes, the words would be the very same, or much more similar.

The like attention to the moods and personal affixes of the verbs is necessary, If you ask an Indian how he expresses, in his language, to *go* or walk, and to illustrate

---

*Vide Schroderi thesaurum Linguae Armenicae

your meaning, point to a person who is walking: he will tell you *pumissoo*, he walks. If to make him understand, you walk yourself, his answer will be *kpumseh*, thou walk-est. If you illustrate your meaning by pointing to the walk of the Indian, the answer will be *npumseh*, I walk. If he take you to mean *go* or *walk*, in the imperative mood, he will answer *pumisseh*, walk thou.

MAHICAN—ENGLISH

Amisque, *a beaver.* [the first syllable scarcely sounded]

Anneh, *to.*

Annuweeweh nemannauwoo, *he is a man of superior excellence or courage.*

Annuweeweh wnissoo, *he is more beautiful.*

Ghusooh, *eight.*

Hkeesque, *eye.*

Hpoon, *winter.*

John uduhwhunuw Peteran, *John he loves him Peter.*

Kahnuh nemannnauwoo, *he is a man of extraordinary excellence or courage.*

Kahnuh wnissoo, *he is very beautiful.*

Kameetseh, *thou eatest.*

Keah, *thou or thee.*

Keauwuh, *ye.*

Keesogh, *the sun.*

Kmattannissauteuh, *you are a coward.*

Kmeetseh, *thou eatest.*

Knisk, *thy hand.*

Kogh, *thy father.*

Kpeesquausooeh, *you are a girl.*

Kpehtuhquisseh, *thou art tall.*

Kpehtuhquissehmuh, *ye are tall.*

Kpumseh, *thou walkest.*

29

Kpumsehmuh, *ye walk.*

Kthuwhunin, *I love thee.*

Ktuhwhunoohmuh, *I love you* (in the plural).

Ktumhecan, *thy hatchet.*

Ktumhecanoowuh, *your hatchet.*

Mannito, *a spirit, a spectre, or any thing frightful.*

Matansautee, *a coward.*

Mattipeh, *sit down.*

Meenuh, *give it him.*

Meetseh, *eat thou.*

Meetsoo, *he eateth.*

Metooque, *wood.*

Mkissin, *shoe.*

Mquoh, *a bear.*

Mtandou, *devil.*

Mtannit, *ten.*

Mtissoo, *he is homely.*

Mtissoo, *an impostor (he is an impostor or bad man).*

Mtit, *good for nought.*

Naughees, *my granchild.*

Nauneeweh, *nine.*

Nauwoh, *four.*

Nbey, *water.*

Nboo, *dead (he is dead).*

Ndinnehnuh, *I run to a place.*

Ndinnoghoh, *I walk to a place.*

Ndiotuwauch wupkoh, *I shall fight to-morrow*.

Ndoghpeh, *I ride*.

Nduhwhuntammin, *I love it*.

Nduhwhununk, *I love them*.

Nduhwhunuw, *I love him or her*.

Ndumhecan, *my hatchet*.

Ndumhecannuh, *our hatchet*.

Neah, *I*.

Neaunuh, *we*.

Neesoh, *two*.

Nemannauk, *men*.

Nemannauw, *man, a man*.

Nemannauwoo, *he is a man*.

Nemeetseh, *I eat*.

Nemoghhome, *my grandfather*.

Nepoo, *dead (he is dead)*.

Netohcon, *an elder brother*.

Ngheesum, *a younger brother, a younger sister*.

Ngwittoh, *one*.

Ngwittus, *six*.

Nip, *to die (I die)*.

Nmase, *an elder sister*.

Nmees, *elder sister*.

Nmeetseh, *I eat*.

Nmeetsehnuh, *we eat*.

Nnisk, *my hand*.

Nochehnuh, *I run from a place*.

Nogh, *my father*.

Noghhoh, *three.*

Noghnuh, *our father.*

Nohhum, *my grandmother.*

Notoghoh, *I walk from a place.*

Npehtuhquisseh, *I am tall.*

Npehtuhquissehnuh, *we are tall.*

Npumseh, *I walk.*

Npumsehnuh, *we walk.*

Nsase, *my uncle by my mother's side.*

Nsconmoo, *he is malicious.*

Nsconmowukon, *malice.*

Nsees, *my uncle.*

Nuchehque, *my uncle by the father's side.*

Nunon, *five.*

Ocheh, *from.*

Oieet, *the man who lives or dwells in a place.*

Oioteet, *the man who fights.*

Paumse-an, *thou walking.*

Paumseauk, *we walking.*

Paumseauque, *ye walking.*

Paumse-cheek, *they walking.*

Paumseecheek, *they who walk.*

Paumseet, *he walking, the man who walks.*

Paumse-uh, *I walking.*

Pautoh, *fetch.*

Peesquausoo, *a girl.*

Pehtuhquessoouk, *they are tall.*

Pehtuhquisseecheek, *the tall men.*

Pehtuhquisseet, *the man who is tall.*

Pehtuhquissoo, *he is tall.*

Penumpausoo, *a boy.*

Penumpausoouk, *boys.*

Peyuhtommauwukon, *religion.*

Pootouwah, *dress the kettle (make a fire).*

Pumisseh, *go, walk thou.*

Pumissoo, *he goes, he walks.*

Pumissoouk, *they walk.*

Sekeenundowukon, *hatred.*

Sepoo, *river.*

Stauw, *fire.*

Tehah, *where.*

Tmohhecan, *a hatchet or ax.*

Towohque, *ear.*

Tuneh, *how.*

Tupouwus, *seven.*

Uhwhundowukon, *love.*

Ukeesquan, *his eyes.*

Unisk, *his hand.*

Utoh, *his heart.*

Utumhecan, *his hatchet.*

Utumhecannoowuh, *their hatchet.*

Uwoh, *he (that man), this man, or this thing.*

Waughecheh, *her husband.*

Waunseet, *the man who is beautiful.*

Weekumuhm, *house.*

Weensis, *his head.*

Weeween, *marry.*

Weghaukun, *hair.*

Wepeeton, *his teeth.*

Wnechun, *his child.*

Wnechunan, *his child.*

Wneeweh, *I thank you.*

Wnissoo, *he is beautiful.*

Wnoghquetookoke, *Stockbridge.*

Wnoghquetookoke ndinnetoghpeh, *I ride to Stockbridge.*

Wnoghquetookoke nochetoghpeh, *I ride from Stockbridge.*

Wnukuwoh ndiotuwoh, *yesterday I fight.*

Wnukuwoh ndiotuwohpoh, *yesterday I fought.*

Wupkauch ndiotuwoh, *to-morrow I fight.*

ENGLISH—MAHICAN

Ax, *tmohhecan*.

Bear, a, *mquoh*.
Beautiful, he is, *wnissoo*. **The man who is beautiful**, *waunseet*. **He is more beautiful**, *annuweeweh wnissoo*. **He is very beautiful**, *kahnuh wnissoo*.
Beaver, a, *amisque*.
Boy, a, *penumpausoo*. **Boys**, *penumpausoouk*.
Brother, an elder, *netohcon*. **A younger Brother**, *ngheesum*.

Child, his, *wnechun, wnechunan*.
Coward, a, *matansautee*. **You are a coward**, *kmattannissauteuh*.

Dead, he is, *nboo or nepoo*.
Devil, *mtandou*.
Die, to, *nip*. **I die**, *nip*.
Dress the kettle (make a fire), *pootouwah*.
Dwells, the man who lives or dwells in a place, *oieet*.

Ear, *towohque*.
Eat, I, *nmeetseh, nemeetseh*. **Thou eatest**, *kmeetseh, kameetseh*. **He eateth**, *meetsoo*. **We eat**, *nmeetsehnuh*. **Eat thou**, *meetseh*.
Eight, *ghusooh*.
Eye, *hkeesque*. **His eyes**, *ukeesquan*.

Father, my, *nogh.* **Thy father,** *kogh.* **Our father,** *nogh-nuh.*

Fetch, *pautoh.*

Fights, the man who, *oioteet.* **Yesterday I fight,** *wnuku-woh ndiotuwoh.* **Yesterday I fought,** *wnukuwoh ndio-tuwohpoh.* **I shall fight to-morrow,** *ndiotuwauch wup-koh.* **To-morrow I fight,** *wupkauch ndiotuwoh.*

Fire, *stauw.*

Five, *nunon.*

Four, *nauwoh.*

Frightful, any thing, *mannito.*

From, *ocheh.*

Girl, a, *peesquausoo.* **You are a girl,** *kpeesquausooeh.*

Give it him, *meenuh.*

Go, *pumisseh.* **He goes,** *pumissoo.*

Good for nought, *mtit.*

Granchild, my, *naughees.*

Grandfather, my, *nemoghhome.*

Grandmother, my, *nohhum.*

Hair, *weghaukun.*

Hand, my, *nnisk.* **Thy hand,** *knisk.* **His hand,** *unisk.*

Hatchet, a, *tmohhecan.* **My hatchet,** *ndumhecan.* **Thy hatchet,** *ktumhecan.* **His hatchet,** *utumhecan.* **Our hatchet,** *ndumhecannuh.* **Your hatchet,** *ktumhecan-oowuh.* **Their hatchet,** *utumhecannoowuh.*

Hatred, *sekeenundowukon.*

He, *uwoh*.
Head, his, *weensis*.
Heart, his, *utoh*.
Homely, he is, *mtissoo*.
House, *weekumuhm*.
How, *tuneh*.
Husband, her, *waughecheh*.

I, *neah*.
Impostor, he is an, *mtissoo*.

Lives, the man who lives or dwells in a place, *oieet*.
Love, *uhwhundowukon*. **I love thee**, *ktuhwhunin*. **I love him or her**, *nduhwhunuw*. **I love it**, *nduhwhuntam-min*. **I love you (in the plural)**, *ktuhwhunoohmuh*. **I love them**, *nduhwhununk*. **John he loves him Peter**, *John uduhwhunuw Peteran*.

Make a fire, *pootouwah*.
Malice, *nsconmowukon*.
Malicious, he is, *nsconmoo*.
Man, a, *nemannauw*. **Men**, *nemannauk*. **He is a man**, *nemannauwoo*. **He is a man of superior excellence or courage**, *annuweeweh nemannauwoo*. **He is a man of extraordinary excellence or courage**, *kahnuh nemannnauwoo*. **Bad man**, *mtissoo*.
Marry, *weeween*.

Nine, *nauneeweh.*

One, *ngwittoh.*

Religion, *peyuhtommauwukon.*

Ride, I, *ndoghpeh.* **I ride to Stockbridge**, *wnoghque-tookoke ndinnetoghpeh.* **I ride from Stockbridge**, *wnoghquetookoke nochetoghpeh.*

River, *sepoo.*

Run, I run to a place, *ndinnehnuh.* **I run from a place**, *nochehnuh.*

Seven, *tupouwus.*

Shoe, *mkissin.*

Sister, an elder, *nmase,* **nmees.** **A younger sister**, *ngheesum.*

Sit down, *mattipeh.*

Six, *ngwittus.*

Spectre, a, *mannito.*

Spirit, a, *mannito.*

Stockbridge, *wnoghquetookoke.*

Sun, the, *keesogh.*

Tall, I am, *npehtuhquisseh.* **Thou art tall**, *kpehtuhquis-seh.* **He is tall**, *pehtuhquissoo.* **We are tall**, *npehtuhquissehnuh.* **Ye are tall**, *kpehtuhquissehmuh.* **They are tall**, *pehtuhquessoouk.* **The man who is tall**, *pehtuhquisseet.* **The tall men**, *pehtuhquisseecheek.*

Teeth, his, *wepeeton.*

Ten, *mtannit.*

Thank you, I, *wneeweh.*

That man, *uwoh.*

Thee, *keah.*

This man, *uwoh.*

This thing, *uwoh.*

Thou, *keah.*

Three, *noghhoh.*

To, *anneh.*

To-morrow I fight, *wupkauch ndiotuwoh.* **I shall fight to-morrow,** *ndiotuwauch wupkoh.*

Two, *neesoh.*

Uncle, my, *nsees.* **My uncle by the father's side,** *nuchehque.* **My uncle by my mother's side,** *nsase.*

Walk, I, *npumseh.* **Thou walkest,** *kpumseh.* **He walketh,** *pumissoo.* **We walk,** *npumsehnuh.* **Ye walk,** *kpumsehmuh.* **They walk,** *pumissoouk.* **Walk thou,** *pumisseh.* **The man who walks,** *paumseet.* **They who walk,** *paumseecheek.* **I walking,** *paumse-uh.* **Thou walking,** *paumse-an.* **He walking,** *paumseet.* **We walking,** *paumseauk.* **Ye walking,** *paumseauque.* **They walking,** *paumse-cheek.* **I walk to a place,** *ndinnoghoh.* **I walk from a place,** *notoghoh.*

Water, *nbey.*

We, *neaunuh.*

Where, *tehah*.
Winter, *hpoon*.
Wood, *metooque*.

Ye, *keauwuh*.
Yesterday I fight, *wnukuwoh ndiotuwoh*.   **Yesterday I fought**, *wnukuwoh ndiotuwohpoh*.

NUMERICAL TABLE

1. Ngwittoh
2. Neesoh
3. Noghhoh
4. Nauwoh
5. Nunon
6. Ngwittus
7. Tupouwus
8. Ghusooh
9. Nauneeweh
10. Mtannit

CLASSIFICATION OF THE EASTERN ALGONQUIAN LANGUAGES

EASTERN ALGONQUIAN

Micmac
Abenakian
    Maliseet-Passamaquoddy
    Eastern Abenaki
    Western Abenaki
Etchemin
Southern New England
    Massachusett-Narragansett
    Loup
    Mohegan-Pequot
    Quiripi-Unquachog
Delawaran
    Mahican
    Munsee Delaware
    Unami Delaware
Nanticoke-Conoy
Virginia Algonquian
    Powhatan
Carolina Algonquian
    Pamlico

Source: Goddard 1996.

45

Also available in the American Language Reprint Series

Volume 1. A Vocabulary of the Nanticoke Dialect
Volume 2. A Vocabulary of Susquehannock
Volume 3. A Vocabulary of the Unami Jargon
Volume 4. A Vocabulary of Powhatan
Volume 5. An Ancient New Jersey Indian Jargon
Volume 6. A Vocabulary of Tuscarora
Volume 7. A Vocabulary of Woccon
Volume 8. A Dictionary of Powhatan
Volume 9. A Vocabulary of Mohegan-Pequot
Volume 10. A Vocabulary of New Jersey Delaware
Volume 11. A Vocabulary of Stadaconan
Volume 12. Denny's Vocabulary of Delaware
Volume 13. A Vocabulary of Roanoke
Volume 14. Denny's Vocabulary of Shawnee
Volume 15. Cummings' Vocabulary of Delaware
Volume 16. Early Vocabularies of Mohawk
Volume 17. Schoolcraft's Vocabulary of Oneida
Volume 18. Elliot's Vocabulary of Cayuga
Volume 19. Schoolcraft's Vocabulary of Onondaga
Volume 20. Elliot's Vocabulary of Mohawk
Volume 21. Cummings' Vocabulary of Shawnee
Volume 22. A Vocabulary of Seneca
Volume 23. The Tutelo Language
Volume 24. Handy's Vocabulary of Miami
Volume 25. Observations on the Mahican Language
Volume 26. Minor Vocabularies of Tutelo and Saponi
Volume 27. Wood's Vocabulary of Massachusett
Volume 28. Chew's Vocabulary of Tuscarora
Volume 29. Early Fragments of Minsi Delaware
Volume 30. A Vocabulary of Wyandot
Volume 31. Heckewelder's Vocabulary of Nanticoke
Volume 32. Minor Vocabularies of Huron
Volume 33. Castiglioni's Vocabulary of Cherokee
Volume 34. Elements of a Miami-Illinois Grammar
Volume 35. Ridout's Vocabulary of Shawnee
Volume 36. A Vocabulary of Stockbridge Mahican
Volume 37. Minor Vocabularies of Nanticoke-Conoy
Volume 39. A Vocabulary of Etchemin
Volume 40. A Vocabulary of the Souriquois Jargon

For more information on the series, see our website at:
www.arxbooks.com/evolpub/ALR/ALRbooks.html

www.ingramcontent.com/pod-product-compliance
Lightning Source LLC
Chambersburg PA
CBHW022031090426
42739CB00006BA/384